OUT
of the
SOUTH

OUT of the SOUTH

poems

Neal Bowers

Louisiana State University Press
baton rouge
2002

Copyright © 1987, 1988, 1989, 1990, 1991, 1992, 1993, 1994, 1995, 1997, 1998, 2001, 2002 by Neal Bowers
All rights reserved
Manufactured in the United States of America
First printing
11 10 09 08 07 06 05 04 03 02
5 4 3 2 1

    Designer: Amanda McDonald Scallan
    Typeface: Sabon
    Printer and binder: Thomson-Shore, Inc.

Library of Congress Cataloging-in-Publication Data:
Bowers, Neal, 1948–
  Out of the South : poems / Neal Bowers.
      p. cm.
  ISBN 0-8071-2818-X (cloth : alk. paper) — ISBN 0-8071-2819-8 (pbk. : alk. paper)
  1. Southern States—Poetry. I. Title.
  PS3552.O8732 O97 2002
  811'.54—dc21

                                  2002006844

The paper in this book meets the guidelines for permanence and durability of the Committee on Production Guidelines for Book Longevity of the Council on Library Resources. ∞

Various poems first appeared, sometimes in slightly different form, in the following publications: *America:* "Remnants"; *Critical Quarterly:* "Different"; *High Plains Literary Review:* "The Secret Place"; *Hudson Review:* "Death Sentence "; "Integrations "; "A Word with My Father"; *Indiana Review:* "The Philosophy of Metaphor"; *Kansas Quarterly:* "Heroics"; *North American Review:* "Black Walnuts"; *Poetry:* "Night Builder "; "Tenth-Year Elegy "; "Minding"; "The Passed "; "Communications "; "Hymns "; "Dead Man Interview "; "For the Ego "; "Flight"; *Sewanee Review:* "Lost in the Vicinity "; "Out of the South"; *Shenandoah:* "The Future "; "Driving Lessons "; "'More Light!'"; "Migratory Patterns "; "Welcome"; *Southern Poetry Review:* "A Legacy "; "Faith"; *Southern Review:* "For the South "; "The Dare"; *Tar River Poetry:* "Addie's Story "; "Dusk"; *Zone 3:* "Singing Dixie "; "Spells "; "Confederates."

To the memory of my mother
   Willine Tigart Bowers
1929–2000

CONTENTS

For the South   1

The Future   2

Singing Dixie   4

Integrations   5

White, U.S.A.   7

Death Sentence   9

Welcome   11

A Legacy   12

Addie's Story   14

Remnants   15

Driving Lessons   16

The Secret Place   18

Lost in the Vicinity   19

The Dare   20

Spells   21

Heroics   22

Faith   23

A Word with My Father   24

Hymns   25

Confederates   27

Dead Man Interview   28

Communications   29

"More Light!"   30

Black Walnuts   31

Night Builder   32

Tenth-Year Elegy   33

Out of the South   34

Different   44

Minding   46

The Passed   47

For the Ego   48

The Philosophy of Metaphor   49

Dusk   50

Flight   51

Migratory Patterns   52

OUT
of the
SOUTH

FOR THE SOUTH

I hate your hills white with dogwood
or pink with redbud in spring
as if you invented hope, as if
in the middle of red clay,
limestone outcroppings,
and oak trees dead with fungus
something slight and beautiful
should make us smile.

I hate the way honeysuckle drapes
fences, blooms in the ditch
where everyone dumps garbage;
the evening air sweet with cedar
and fields of burley;
the way irises and buttercups
mark the old dimensions of a house
destroyed a hundred years ago;
how a span of Queen Anne's lace
rocks the whole moon, and the sumac
runs dark against the hill.

I hate the drawl, the lazy voice
saying I've been away so long
I sound like I'm from nowhere;
the old hand gathering snowballs or peonies
or forking up an extra dish of greens,
bitter, just the way I like them.

THE FUTURE
(Detroit, 1950)

Because the jobs were there
and a man could get rich
working on the line, the South
retreated north to Michigan,
whole families eating crackers and baloney
by the side of the road,
changing drivers to keep
moving through corn fields
and foreign towns,
sundown and darkness,
the moon a prophecy of chrome,
the stars 10 million headlights
of the cars they would build.

Ahead lay a city bright with steel;
behind, the dark fields folded
over everything they knew;
and when they dozed
on cramped back seats, they dreamed
such dreams as the road can make,
of drifting on a lake or stream
or lying down in hay to dream of traveling,
so that when they woke to a bump,
a cough, a voice saying, "It's your turn,"
they were lost to themselves
and took a few moments
to remember their names.

Mostly behind their backs,
the locals called them
rednecks, crackers, goddamned rebs.
Strange to be strange,
in their new neighborhoods,
to be ethnic with a thick accent
and a taste for food the grocers didn't stock—
hog jowl and blackeyes, turnip greens,
roasting ears, souse-meat—
the butcher shrugging,

the produce man shaking his head.
Sometimes their own voices
took them by surprise,
sounding odd and out of place
in the din of a city bus, ringing
lost in the evening air when
they called their children in for supper.

At work they touched
parts of tomorrow,
next year's models always
taking shape and vanishing,
the present obsolete, the past
merely a rumor,
all hours blurring
into one continuous moment
of finishing a fragment,
each piece the same piece,
movements identical,
endless, like a punishment in hell.

No way out but back
to their old lives, a future
they already knew by heart,
a few on the road each month
in cars they may have helped assemble,
tokens of their failed success,
legacies for boys to find
years later rusting on some lot,
banged up but still a dream
and fast enough when overhauled
to make them feel they could blast
straight into tomorrow,
as they raced their engines at each stoplight
and cruised their towns in circles.

SINGING DIXIE

Old times there are not forgotten
when each spring's elm sprouts
have to be tugged out
of flower beds and fence rows,
everyone down in the back
from so much straining,
wondering where the seeds come from,
the double-row canopy
that tunneled Franklin Avenue
chopped down thirty years ago,
old-timers remembering a shade so dense
sparrows roosted by midafternoon
and a good, hard rain
would barely wet the street.

Strange how something so diseased
hangs on amid the buttercups,
roots firm in a clump of peonies,
in neighborhoods white with dogwood,
where our parents taught us
some people should remember their place
and my brother repeats the lesson
for his kids beginning school.
Look away. Look away.

INTEGRATIONS

I don't even know his name,
but I remember what we called him—
"High Pockets"—a slur right out of vaudeville
and the venom of our hearts,
because we knew his black face
wasn't painted on with cork.

"High Pockets, lawdy boy, don't you
lose yo'self at night?" And then the hooting
and someone saying, "Dumbass nigger,"
but he just kept on walking
down the halls of Clarksville High
while I hung back and snickered.

The only other black, a girl, we left alone,
letting her pass in silence down our gauntlet
of eyes, playing the southern gentlemen,
though someone whispered, "The blacker the berry
the sweeter the juice," and someone else said,
"Once you go black you'll never go back."

While we scorned them, they changed everything,
like dye dropped on a slide in biology,
making our true souls as visible as single cells,
each holding a dark nucleus,
our recurrent blot of sin, contained,
passed on, and merged in our sick medium.

At home, my parents grumbled,
"Two more years and you would have been clear.
Why couldn't they wait two more years?"
And they talked about place over supper,
about knowing your place in this world,
while I took seconds and kept on eating.

Not for the accident of birth,
the casual chance of place and time,
not for these my lifelong punishment,
but for the deliberate act,

the cur trained first inside the heart
to clamp down hard and hold.

When he sat down at my table, I was ready,
legs flexed to move
to the far side of the lunchroom—
no words, just a loud display,
the ugliness of gesture
and my own crude segregation.

With the white wall at my back,
I held my ground and watched him
eat alone in the middle of a long table,
never looking up from his plate
as we clattered and mumbled around him
and ate our bitterness and liked it.

This is the moment that damns:
the boy I was in 1963, proud in his white isolation,
forever looking out at me with my own eyes,
hands clenched hard above a plate,
food like gravel in his mouth,
his heart, now hidden in my heart, hammering.

Out in the open, he wears my changed face,
thinks my thoughts, says he's sorry—
even writes this to prove it—
the same one who was too good
to eat with "High Pockets" and to this day
doesn't know his name.

In the dark wake of years I cling to him,
that boy I was whose hate could drown us both,
kicking hard to stay afloat, knowing
there's no way to save just one of us.

WHITE, U.S.A.

White is nobody's home,
is, in fact, an absence,
the end of the line
where the lost bags go,
the misdirected trunks
crammed with sheets and hoods
stacked on the edge
of undiluted emptiness,
population zero
and no welcome sign,
a purity that endures forever
because it purges everything,
pogrom of the atomic particle,
not even air to breathe,
a pallid vacuum.

How is it then I remember
Saturdays as pinkwhite as hibiscus,
Mama and her blackberry cobbler,
Daddy asking for seconds,
the billboard by the river
saying, "I may be black,
but I's clean as Richardson's coal,"
the buses with "Colored in Rear,"
and the black balcony above us
at the matinee?

Which side of the street
am I crossing to when I cross
to avoid the black kids
moving in a smoke of music?
Why do I always feel guilty
in chess if I draw white,
if I draw black,
if I play both sides of the board,
myself against myself, thinking,
"Okay, you bigoted son of a bitch,
I've got you cornered now,"
knowing I heard myself think that
and can stalemate every game?

By night, I am stitching
the eye-holes closed,
bleaching the bloodstains
and bleaching them again,
so much linen
to transform back into itself,
each morning a hopeless tangle.

DEATH SENTENCE

We knew we'd find him guilty
and would have saved the state
the time of proving the obvious
if we could have waved our hands
the way a dozen people sipping coffee
might stop a story they've heard more often
than complaints about the weather,
a slow erasure on the air,
because there was the look of him,
an aimlessness, as if he meant to go
nowhere and everywhere all at once,
a kind of random certainty,
as when a tornado wobbles into town
and obliterates a house without lifting
a shingle on the roof next door
and people say, "the will of God,"
having no other explanation
for their luck or their lives,
wanting to be blessed or damned
since either means being chosen,
and anything is better than finding
your walls blown down or a stranger
waiting in an unlit corner without reason,
which is why not knowing why he did it
only made us more determined
to convict him, his innocent plea
merely another layer on our resolve,
though he must have sensed
how grateful we would be,
not so much for an admission of guilt
as for an explanation, a light
turned on at last
in that chamber of the heart
where violence polishes the cutlery
like a compulsive butler,
a frightening formality
suggesting something like purpose,
a rational brutality we understood
as we studied his face

and imagined it hooded in the chair
plugged in to kingdom-come,
which for him would be hell, of course,
and I confess I thought
about what it would feel like
to throw the switch myself,
a soft flexing of the wrist
as when pulling down a window shade,
a smooth glide waving him
into that sizzling darkness
he deserved for being what he was,
not one of us but something foul,
a thing that shouldn't be allowed
to waste the air, no matter how well
his lawyer dressed him, cut his hair,
drilled him on etiquette,
as if a rotted soul could be concealed
with a necktie and cologne,
all of us gagging on the stench,
thinking, "Welcome to our slaughterhouse,
you son-of-a-bitch," the judge's hammer
falling hard on his head
when we finally gave the signal,
putting an end to the formalities
and the time-wasting niceties of justice,
his walking carcass led away
for the last time, for the last time
his evil face grinning back at us
as if he knew something we didn't know.

WELCOME

"American by Birth,
Southern by the Grace of God"—
all that on the front of a baseball cap
pulled low to hide his bleary eyes,
my cousin, proud in his drunkenness,
has come to see how I look and sound
now that I'm Yankeefied,
while in the kitchen, my mother fries chicken
and sings, happy to have family
around her table,
and I'm thinking something about
the old calamity of the blood,
trying to remember whose phrase it is—
or if it's mine—and then the irony
of a mockingbird's racket in the dogwood
just outside the window, with cousin asking,
"What's so funny?" forgetting he's not in a bar,
his flushed face challenging,
my fists unconsciously clenching, ready
to knock him off his chair,
until he laughs,
looking for the first time as if he knows me.

A LEGACY

In the photo I've never seen,
she holds baby great-grandfather,
braids hanging over her shoulders.
I think she's beautiful,
though my mother,
who tells me what she was told,
says only "full-blooded Cherokee,"
under her breath, as if swearing
at a spot that won't come out,
claims the cousin who owns the picture
won't show it anymore,
may have thrown it away
with a load of old shoes
and closet clutter.

Because white turns the whole spectrum away,
it is the color of absence,
a condition defined by what it's not,
as in "We are not Indians."
Strange to hear my relatives
who have so little wanting even less,
mistaking emptiness for the brimful cup,
the whole Irish-English lot of them,
dirt-poor and southern-proud
for who they think they are,
only one generation away
from hired hands and sharecroppers,
only three away from the woman in the picture.
The younger ones hang Confederate flags
above their beds, bolt "Forget, Hell!" plates
to their cars and trucks, forgetting.

To save anything from oblivion,
it must be named
and called into the world.
Old grandmother, I name you now
and call you out of my own need,
a name that sounds like weeping but means
leaves on a still morning,

or the silence after rain.
Buried once for death
and once for who you were,
your second grave deeper,
lower than love and under memory,
you have withstood tons of darkness,
waiting, compressed to brilliance.

I can see, in my mother's face,
the face I've never seen in the old picture,
sharp-boned, stern, but with a softness
in the eyes, a tender patience—
or maybe I imagine this,
the blood so distant and diluted.
For my own portion,
I have the true inheritance,
the disease that proves the lineage,
diabetes, skipping generations,
killing my grandfather at 35,
a dependable randomness
pointing you . . . not you . . . me.
Overtaken by the past
in the middle of my life,
I have finally become mortal,
feeling in my veins the blood
of a fallen race.

Sometimes, when it's late and the body
lies down with itself,
wanting a better truce with death
than this balance on a needlepoint,
she waves from the dark rim,
webbed in a sweet fatigue,
and calls me by the name
I answer to in dreams,
and I answer.

ADDIE'S STORY
(Addie Darnell Bowers, 1891–1981)

Nearly sick myself from sitting up so long
to nurse a dying man, I went home
and sunk in feather comforters,
the goose-down mattress holding me
like a butter mold,
sleep setting in with its sweet clabber,
while three miles down the road
John Barnette lay where I left him,
floating face up in a pool of quilts
and delirious for my fried chicken,
unable to swallow broth
or even a tablespoon of water;
and I had calmed him saying,
"Yes, yes, my best young fryer—
tomorrow, I promise, tomorrow,"
those same words swinging later in my mind
like an amulet for sleep,
my husband's breath a soft clock
on the pillow beside me,
the whole farm charmed and heavy-lidded,
humming with fatigue,
a dull drone under consciousness
that sometime in the night changed pitch,
climbed into a moan, then a wail
like the shrill of steel on steel,
the mules kicking loose from the barn,
running round and round on their hind legs,
hens all down from their rafters
and scattered through the trees
and lilac shrubs as if a storm
had blown them there or they had flown
from a terrible slaughter,
and I knew John Barnette was dead.

REMNANTS

Winding a mile or more
through fields and hills,
weeds raking fenders,
wheels doing a slow-motion gallop
out of holes and over stones, we were
riding against the grain of time,
backward to my mother's first home.

Guided by a grove of trees, a bend
in the stream she thought she remembered,
we left the car, descended
to a dry creek bed,
wrack of gravel and boulders
silent as a ruin of monuments.

Looking for evidence,
she found a hinge nailed to an oak,
half healed over in the bark,
two rusted strands of wire, a second growth
of apple trees, wild and spindly
in a thicket of nettle and briars.
Where the front yard must have been,
a clump of irises struggled through weeds.

Wanting a chimney-stone,
a piece of glass, anything
to take away to show
where she had been,
to make her life more real,
the vanishing present bearable,
she stooped beside the irises,
all blades and out of bloom,
for a picture that shows her
huddled like a child at play
on her own front lawn,
whispering to the vacant air,
"I once lived here."

DRIVING LESSONS

I learned to drive in a parking lot
on Sundays, when the stores were closed—
slow maneuvers out beyond the light-poles,
no destination, just the ritual of clutch and gas,
my father clenching with the grinding gears,
finally giving up and leaving my mother
to buck and plunge with me and say,
repeatedly, "Once more. Try just once more."

She walked out on him once
when I was six or seven, my father
driving beside her, slow as a beginner,
pleading, my baby brother and I
crying out the windows, "Mama, don't go!"
It was a scene to break your heart
or make you laugh—those wailing kids,
a woman walking briskly with a suitcase,
the slow car following like a faithful dog.

I don't know why she finally got in
and let us take her back
to whatever she had made up her mind to leave;
but the old world swallowed her up
as soon as she opened that door,
and the other life she might have lived
lay down forever in its dark infancy.

Sometimes, when I'm home, driving
through the old neighborhoods, stopping
in front of each little house we rented,
my stillborn other life gets in,
the boy I would have been if
my mother had kept on walking.
He wants to be just like her,
far away and gone forever, wants
me to press down on the gas;
but however fast I squeal away,
the shaggy past keeps loping behind,
sniffing every turn.

When I stop in the weedy parking lot,
the failed stores of the old mall
make a dark wall straight ahead;
and I'm alone again, until my parents get in,
unchanged after all these years,
my father, impatient, my mother
trying hard to smile, waiting for me
to steer my way across this emptiness.

THE SECRET PLACE

After thirty years, I find the spot again,
my bucket clacking in tall weeds—
galvanized five-gallon pail
with a handle that creaks
at every arm-swing—
same kind my father carried
on mornings like this one
into which I would pour
what I picked in my coffee can.

In the middle of the thicket
he moved so fast
his berries drummed like hail,
then shushed as the bottom was covered,
a dark accumulation soft as sleep,
sweet harvesting,
drone of June bugs,
honeysuckle pouring everywhere.

Now there's only cedar scrub and sumac
and a sun that marks an old point
in the sky, like a mockery.
Not to go back empty,
I find some fossils, drop them in.
They prove a sea was here.

LOST IN THE VICINITY

Late summer twilight, and I have dozed
over my book into a childhood game
of kick-the-can, someone calling my name
across the dimming lawn, my mother, maybe,
saying it's time to come inside;
but when I open my eyes, the voice continues,
pleading on the street outside my window,
and the name is "Rusty" or "Dusty," almost a song,
each syllable sustained and quavering,
and then a pause, and then the name again—
"Rusty." "Dusty."
He is just a boy, not used to losing things,
and cups both hands around his mouth
when he sings, aiming his one word
into the darkness, into the silent neighborhood
where we stand watching him, house by house,
as all the lost companions of our lives come home.

THE DARE

He climbed the flaking girders, and jumped—
no talk, no hesitation, just a quick spring
into midnight air, a faint splash,
and then the frantic voices calling his name
out over the river and the dark sound it made.

My brother was there, and two of his friends,
wild with their 17 years of small-town life,
of being known as their fathers' sons.

The limestone bluffs alone answered,
giving back their thin voices; and the wind
made a low moan on the bridge
as they began to plead with the river,
the night, bargaining for time,
for a future they had taken for granted.

When he finally walked into their headlights,
wet and smeared with mud, a rope of algae
in his hair, they began to laugh;
and whatever he had wanted to say
was lost in the jokes coming fast.

So he joined in and bragged
how he had kicked death in the ass,
and they all drove back to town,
shouting and flashing their lights,
running down the night
that fell under their wheels
and rose whole again behind them.

SPELLS

To keep him from swallowing his tongue,
we learned how to pin it with a thumb
and let it writhe, a lively mussel
tugging to enter the darker cave
where something groaned, wounded
and terribly alone.

But we couldn't stop his eyes
from looking up into his brain,
reading the black intelligence,
his lolled head rolling and bobbing,
cradled in our hands or in a lap
above the floor.

Whenever he went down on his knees
or fell like someone struck by lightning,
twitching everywhere at once,
our whole world shuddered,
shifted along the great fault
running through our lives.

Kneeling beside him, we prayed
and pleaded, burned bay leaf
in a tea cup, rubbed his temples
with mineral oil, held a cold cloth
to his forehead and called his name
over the rumbling.

Some of us confessed our sins out loud,
repented every deed and thought,
bartered what few goods we had
to win him back another time,
his wide eyes empty but quickly
filling with the broken world.

HEROICS

If I were a child, I could convince myself
these needles make me special, not just different
but brave, as if I volunteered.

Sometimes I feel absurd,
middle-aged and sitting on the edge of the bathtub,
a roll of fat pinched up, syringe poised like a dart.

What I have came from my grandfather,
dead long before I was born,
his last days comatose, breath sweet as a cider press.

I think of him sometimes, as the dose goes in—
how little might have saved him—a poor man
needing medicine, proud until the end.

Here, the faucet drips into the bathroom sink.
I noticed it this morning in the moment's
hesitation before plunging the needle in;

and I know he did what he had to do; the myth
came later: of his Herculean heart
propping the wall so long against an ocean.

FAITH

And when I passed by thee, and saw thee polluted in thine own blood, I said unto thee when thou was in thy blood, Live: yea, I said unto thee, when thou was in thy blood, Live.
—Ezekiel 16:6

I said it three times
with my head tipped back,
but the passage I memorized
for nosebleeds didn't work,
and I sat swallowing my lost life,
until someone brought ice
or a cold, wet cloth.

Laid out flat as a cadaver,
I had time to consider
my lack of faith,
the mustard seed I didn't have,
whose absence swelled,
bloomed red on my best shirt.

My old aunts shook their heads
and prayed for me, seeing
in those abstract stains
a boy in danger, tested
and found wanting
in a wilderness of doubt.

When they helped me stand again,
the whole world wobbled underfoot,
the air a thin stratosphere,
and I saw constellations
swirling on my chest,
star-trails tracking
through a bright infinity,
heard with my own ears
the great onrushing noise
of everything, pulse and push,
the outward urge of planets,
of my chasing blood,
and I believed.

A WORD WITH MY FATHER

Cerulean is a word my father never knew.
He would have scoffed at it and said, "Say blue
if you mean blue." Well, I mean blue,
but I mean cerulean, too,
because it has the sky in it, shot through
with sunlight; and the sound of cerulean soothes
the way blue, however elongated, cannot do.
Even my father would say this is true,
were the rules of silence less strict at Riverview,
where the sky in November is a particular blue.

HYMNS

Unbending the shape of the pew
from their backs and shuffling
the pooled blood from their feet,
the congregation stood
and seemed almost to dance,
trying on their singing voices
like indifferent weather,
every song a drizzle
until the cloudburst chorus,
all those voices one downpour
to wash the gullies free
of weed-entangled trash,
to make salvation rise everywhere
like steam.

Through all this splash
and loud cascade,
my father's drought continued,
Sunday to Sunday,
and although he faked by holding
one-half of the hymnal for my mother,
looking down as if
balancing a platter of water,
no note ever passed his lips.

We never spoke of his charade,
but I would watch him, sidelong,
wondering if he heard his purest voice
inside, perfect because unuttered,
an angel strain soaring over
the wash and wrack of Baptist song,
an easy grace embellishing the air;

or did his inner ear hold
memories of something worse—
the groaning of old boards
under tremendous weight, the screech
a nail makes when it's pulled—
the tuneless voice of collapse
and disassembly coming from his throat?

Either way, he balanced
at the edge of music, filled
with his potential—glorious, horrible—
the way God must have leaned out
over the limitless void, before the beginning,
withholding the word that was everything.

CONFEDERATES

My father was only two in 1915
when he sat on Walter Denton's lap
and heard the old man dragging in
his heavy chain of breath, each link
stuttering down the back of his throat.
"Floyd," he whispered, saying the baby's name
like a question, "look yere,"
and he placed my father's hand
on a scar the color of moonlight,
a shrapnel wound from the Yankee boats
that shelled Ft. Donelson.
Then both of them began to cry,
there in the ladderback chair
someone had dragged into elm shade,
away from the stifling house,
until a woman came and saved them
from each other, leaving one
to go into the past and disappear,
the other to follow by way of the future.

DEAD MAN INTERVIEW

Dead for twelve minutes, the plumber in Akron
has a tale to tell the newspapers,
of figures beckoning in a haze of light—
and he's never even heard of Blake or Dante.
Archetypes, the experts say, or the brain's
own chemistry, the final fireworks
before shutting down, like the great display
out over the harbor at the end of summer.

Knowing my father can settle this dispute,
I call him back for half an hour,
choosing twilight, the hinged sky almost shut,
and place him on the back steps smoking, studying
the space between himself and everything else,
something like a surf roaring between us
the way it always did those summer nights,
the minutes passing like limestone dripping
in a cave that will finally seal itself.

I want to know if the dying see more
than the poor brain guttering in a black cup,
and I want it straight from someone who didn't turn back;
but my father doesn't know he's dead,
inhabits just these moments willed for him;
and anyway, he can say only what I have him say,
so he tells me it's all right,
as he did years ago, standing in the open door
with the light pouring in behind him.

COMMUNICATIONS

Sent in after new ground was taken,
my father ducked from ditch to shell-hole,
unwinding the telephone cable behind him,
a pfc. cast as Mercury, connecting
the gods with the lesser gods.

Funny to think of him trailing
the complex filament of speech,
that man, neither shy nor sullen,
who answered only "Yes," "No," "Maybe,"
and never volunteered a private thought.

Standing off with his hands in his pockets
or cupping a cigarette, he seemed to be waiting
with the great rural patience of fields
for whatever might rise pure and nameless
or fall from the sky beyond explanation.

If anyone asked what he was thinking,
he said, "Nothing," and when he died
he rushed out leaving everything unsaid,
uncoiling a dark line into darkness
down which a familiar silence roars.

"MORE LIGHT!"
—Goethe

Suppose those last words
were not a desperate request
but a stunned exclamation,
death a door flung open
into a dark that dazzled
like sun on water.

And what of those other last words,
unfamous in the dry mouth
of an aunt after surgery,
someone holding her papery hand;
or the stranger pulled
from the roadside wreck?

What of those dying alone,
their revelations spoken into emptiness,
into air, the way my father died
at the foot of the hill
below his garden of blueberries?

In the years since his death,
I've remembered those times
the house went dark and he
stumbled blind down basement stairs,
nothing visible, not even his feet
lifted beneath him like flippers under water,
and my mother called above him
where we all huddled together
to ask if he was all right,
and suddenly the air was luminous.

BLACK WALNUTS

The year my father used the car for hulling
was the best. We cobbled the drive
with walnuts gathered in baskets
and cardboard boxes, then rode with him
down that rough lane, forward and backward,
time and again, until the air was bitter to breathe
and the tires spun in the juice.
For years after, every piece of gravel
was dyed brown, and the old Ford
out on the open road would warm up
to a nutty smell, especially in winter
with the windows closed and the heater blowing.

Crouched over hulls mangled green and yellow,
we picked out corrugated shells
even the car's weight couldn't crack
and spread them on the grass to dry.
My father, on his hands and knees, happy
over windfall, talked of how good
the tender meats would taste; and in that moment
I wished with all my heart that he might live forever,
as leaves ticked down around us
and the fresh stain darkened on our hands.

NIGHT BUILDER

He works every night after work, my father,
down in the damp where the furnace sleeps summer away
and the water heater clatters from too much lime.
His muffled hammering so soft and far away
is a dog barking miles off in the woods;
his sawing is an owl.

Lying in the dark
beside an open window, I know
he is making it true,
smoothing out the splinters,
polishing the knots,
sanding me to sleep with a "hush,"
with a "hush."

TENTH-YEAR ELEGY

Careless man, my father,
always leaving me at rest-stops,
coffee shops, some wide spot in the road.
I come out, rubbing my hands on my pants
or levitating two foam cups of coffee,
and can't find him anywhere,
those banged-up fenders gone.

It's the trip itself that blinds him,
black highway like a chute
leading to the mesmerizing end,
his hands locked dead on the wheel
and following, until he misses me,
steers wide on the graveled shoulders,
turns around.

This time he's been gone so long
I've settled in here—married,
built a house, planted trees for shade
stopped waiting to see him pull into the drive—
though the wind sometimes makes a highway roar
high up in the branches, and I stop
whatever I am doing and look up.

OUT OF THE SOUTH

Back home on the sly, as usual,
one more night in the Riverview Ramada,
en route somewhere else like any other traveler,
with no time for the relatives,
I am dodging every glint of recognition,
keeping an eye out for my brother,
not worrying about my mother
who is home worrying about me.
Whatever I am here to see, maybe to find,
is something needing my single concentration—
no time for distillations of the blood,
small hours in small rooms
fidgety with catch-up conversation,
the voice too weak to make a bridge
over all those years: So how've you been?

Slumped low in the seat of the rental car,
I am anonymous in my hometown—
Clarksville, Tennessee,
Queen City of the Cumberland,
or so the Chamber of Commerce used to boast,
neglecting that other, smaller river,
the Red, which empties itself
at the foot of New Providence hill
and is obliquely commemorated by a mall
called Two Rivers, a name sounding
vaguely Native American, by accident,
now driven down its own trail of tears
by development on the other side of town.

From high ground
near my father's grave in Riverview
where the stones back up
to the old hospital where I was born,
I can see the empty parking lot
and the spot beyond, where the Red
meets the Cumberland and both flow on,
a view not worth having
over the tarred and graveled rooftops

of a dozen businesses and Riverside Drive's
four lanes of steady traffic.
On the opposite hill, across the river
and invisible in trees, is the spot
where most of Valentine Sevier's family
were massacred by the Indians,
according to the old history books,
while participating in an imperialist venture
for capital gain, according to the newer versions.
And I can as easily imagine Valentine
looking back from his outpost
as I can conjure my father
from the packed clay and brittle grass,
the two of them in silent colloquy,
sentinels on separate hills,
across the converging rivers.

If I am ever to have a vision,
this must be the place, so much
of my own blood has leached into this soil,
headstones set up like old-fashioned radios
to blast a name at me wherever I stand
looking down at the groundswell of grandmother,
grandfather, uncle, aunt, cousin,
and God knows how many unmarked kin.
The Cherokee and anyone else not white
were given other ground
to homestead for eternity, a rule still observed
on both sides of the color line.
I have been there, too, out Seven Mile Ferry Road,
where the view is less panoramic,
but where the dead segregate the living
in a way that feels as familiar as family.
Once, when I was a grown boy, I came home
with a clump of mistletoe broken
from a tree in the black graveyard;
and my parents wagged their heads
and said not to go back there again,
which made the sprigs I hung

above the doorway for Christmas
seem dangerous and pagan,
and I lay down each night thinking
of where a kiss might lead
with such dark magic overhead,

If ever a vision is to come,
it must wing in steep past the old cedars
whose musk is a mingling of the dead
in Riverview and strike me here
at sundown when the rooftop of a barn
flashes once in slow motion
in the bottomland across the river
and then goes out like a sleeper's light.
I hear the sexton clang the upper gate
and wait for him to find me
brushing the dry clippings from a footstone
that says Father, the light failing,
and still no vision,
just the memory of being six
and waiting at the roadside gate
for the evening bus that took my grandmother
from her job at the shirt factory in Clarksville
back home to Dover: always a wave
and on Fridays a package hurled from the window,
a shirt or a few marbles wrapped in cloth,
one time a matchbox with two quarters,
one for me and one for my little brother,
a treasure we never found in the ditch
brimful with weeds and rainwater.
I think of it there still, buried
by years of sediment and roadwork,
an unwilling investment in the past.
Too late to ask for my money back,
my grandmother over there
with her elbow cocked inside her coffin,
ready for flinging another surprise
but locked forever in that posture of giving,
the bus rushing on without her.

This is the harmless stuff of memory,
a moment dusted off and shining,
not the whole room of a day
in the house of who we were
when all of us were up in the dark,
my mother setting out for another day
of fancy-stitching at Acme Boot Company—
piece-work, she called it,
turning out as much as she could,
a basketful of eagle wings on leather,
never enough time to make enough—
my father with his armload of candy,
stocking the vending machines at Ft. Campbell,
bringing in the sugar to make the army run.
Whatever my brother and I know of work
we learned from the heavy-bodied shuffle
of our parents setting out each day
and coming home each night to drop
snug in their beds like sacks of shot.
Never awake past 10 P.M., they slept
slotted together like bunkmates in a cell,
as we listened from the other room
to my father's snoring snatches—
held breath and then the loud outrush
of air he seemed unwilling to give up.

If there is such a thing as vision,
it must come now, in the near-darkness
beside my father's grave,
where I could doze into my own apnea
and lurch awake with the breath leaving
and then inhale the freshest wind
like one who has died and been reborn
into the same body, the same place,
with a different face and name.

But when I rise at the sound of the sexton's voice,
I am only myself, chastened by the hour
for lingering too long among the graves,

led to the lower gate, where I hear
the chain pulled through the bars.
Shambling downhill,
the only one to escape
death's lockup this night, I am
stopped on the vacant street by the scent
of something sweet and leading—
honeysuckle bunched and spilling
over the chainlink fence
a messenger sent after me,
the darkening air hung with the herald
of a thousand trumpets, white and yellow,
their one note rich enough to taste,
lodged in my throat where a word
might form an answering blossom,
though nothing comes
all the way downhill to my parked car,
traffic hiding the sound of the merging rivers.

I claim, then, as my legacy
the honeysuckle smelled by my mother
when she was a girl in the rundown
row of houses by the river
where her older brother drowned.
The ruins of her childhood
I excavate—the old roadbed
and the filled-in foundations—
the vacated past, an emptiness
where the lost voice is deadened
by dirt and toppled walls.
I conjure her already two years fatherless,
a girl of eight, barefoot and wise
in the ways of survival,
her own mother gone wild
in young widowhood, gone off
for months with no promise of return,
leaving four small children alone,
in the summer of the year
Robert Lowell pitched a tent

barely a mile upriver on the lawn of Benfolly
and soaked up the ambiance of Tate and Gordon.
From the hilltop above her abandonment
the mansion was just in view on its bluff,
though my mother may never have climbed
to look at it or dream herself across,
nor does her name appear
in any of the famous biographies.
Today, it is called Riverview,
disregarding the cemetery's prior claim,
and I drive there as to a graveyard annex,
my headlights sweeping the darkened windows,
the old house still as a mausoleum
as I turn the circle driveway and stop,
hearing a dog bark somewhere in the woods,
feeling the loneliness of the place.
Pretending to knock at the door,
I wander around to the river side
and look out over the lights of Clarksville,
thinking not of Lowell
rusticating on the lawn of eminence,
but of my mother, her small life
made smaller from this height.
Sitting where the young poet sat
watching the barges pass at night
with their loads of coal and sand,
their headlights swinging bank to bank
like the beam of someone searching,
I could lie back on the grass and sleep,
such a peaceful resignation has come over me,
but not a vision, nothing rising or descending,
no voice calling me out of myself.
Still, there is a strange alignment here,
the sound of canvas flapping in the wind
a ripple of ghostly voices from the house,
my own breath thick as a wrist in my throat
as I think of my mother in her girlhood
and the poets risen into the trees across the river
where they pretend to be eagles.

Whatever I came back for was not this,
not this time-warp feeling of betrayal—
not that anyone chooses who lives the sooty life
of scraped knees and pilfered kindling
or who sits down to make a poem.
Mother, by your little fire on Front Street,
in the house with the trap door
that let out your mother's common-law husband
when the law came looking
and he dragged himself down the bank
and lay in the weeds until they left,
then came back like a furious rat,
you didn't know the poets were working
late into the night, making it rhyme, making it true.
You couldn't have guessed I would make
this ragged return to my hometown and yours,
looking for the vision no one ever finds by looking,
finding your open-ended dates
on the stone above my father, blank granite
at the end of the chiseled hyphen.
To explain why I visit your empty grave
more often than I visit you
would take more than a mansion of poets.

A flash in the downhill brush
and then the rush of fire,
a spire like the bright bole of a tree
jump-starts the darkness
which is suddenly everywhere,
and I am moving toward the glow
without thinking, going sideways
down the bluff, handed along
by saplings and limber branches,
making a small applause of gravel
as it landslides ahead of me and clatters
onto the limestone plateau
where a man is kicking sand
onto a small campfire and muttering
he's on his way,

mistaking me for the owner
come to run him off.
Laboring for breath, I say Wait,
Wait, but the fire is out
and he is shambling away.
I want him to be cordial and wise,
telling me how he set out on the river
years ago in search of some place
and then found the journey itself
was what he had been looking for;
offer up a tin plate of beans,
a cup of boiled coffee and muse
that life is the vision,
the day-by-day of it so astonishing
the only way we can believe it
is to tell ourselves how ordinary it is,
but he is now only leaf-rustle
somewhere in the night.
Stirring the embers he left,
I pitch on twigs and sycamore bark
until the fire returns,
a low flame doubled on the water,
the water rocking between its banks,
the slumberous rocking.

Whether a dream portends anything
depends upon the need for dreaming.
Mine comes as I curl on limestone
and is formed by the wash of the river
giving the sensation of motion,
though I can feel the steady rock
cold under my hip and shoulder
as I go under, and longer,
a numb, dead presence
standing on my shadow
while I stand at an open door
to see my father typing.
He doesn't notice me, even when
I move into the room to look

over his shoulder at the empty page
he tries furiously to fill with letters
the way a child pretends to type
or play piano on the edge of a table,
his hands lifted high
and falling like sparrow hawks,
the keys clattering and jamming
and dropping back into their slots,
everything he has to say colliding
at the brink of expression.
He leaves without speaking,
and when I sit down to type a note
for him, a simple line or two
to say I understand, the typewriter
becomes a boulder, my fingers dumb
against the blunt limestone
I find myself fingering as a mockingbird
wakes me at first light on the cold bluff
and I become myself again,
climb to my car and drive across the river.

Which side you are on is all that matters
in this place, where some families
have handed down stories of Yankee gunboats
anchored in the river, ready to shell the town
if the occupation seemed in jeopardy;
where White Only seemed, even in my lifetime,
an ordinary sign, like Entrance
or Welcome, which didn't mean everyone;
where my parents made a life for us
with their lives and kept to their place
on the working-class side
in one rental house or another;
where the only books in our home
were the Bible and a set of encyclopedias
some salesman fobbed off on my mother,
who wanted her sons to go farther
than she had been able to go,
so she meant to give us the world;

where I ran as a boy and pretended
I was Wilma Rudolph breaking
the finish-line tape,
ashamed to have such thoughts,
not because I was a boy
but because I was white,
proud of her just the same,
of the speed that carried her
down the world's ellipse,
out of our shared hometown.

Sneaking home, to find what was never there—
some kind of wholeness, maybe—
my sundered heart wanting to be healed;
sneaking out again without even phoning
to say good-bye, now that it's too late,
I have betrayed everyone, including myself.
In the hotel parking lot, someone calls my name—
one last chance for vision—some old friend,
a relative, or someone like me back incognito;
but I don't stop, not even when I hear it called
again blurred by the engine whine,
a voice that could be my mother's
or my father's, his ghost having wandered over
from the hillside outpost where he awaits my visits.
Without looking in the mirror, I pull out
and join the morning traffic,
headed somewhere else.

DIFFERENT

Every life is a series of lives.
This he knew, or believed he knew,
which was the same thing
as far as he could tell,
since what we believe to be true
is true, and what we do not believe
fizzles on the synapses, evaporates,
or appears at the corner of the eye
as a little tear for the sleeve
to blot away.
So he thought of himself,
not as a set of nesting selves,
each within another and smaller,
back to some single cell
or invisible point of origin,
but as separate identities
on the continuum of history,
strangers who somehow hold
memories of other selves
that are and are not them,
that person gassed on the picket line,
shouting "Hell no we won't go!"
receding at light-speed from this one,
feet up on the ottoman, dozing, recalling
himself struck down at the edge of a field
by what he thought at first to be a shot,
full in the face, his right cheek stinging,
his own blood a siren in his ears,
then his quick breath stuttering
and the birds again, the wind,
the slow awareness,
his fingers feeling for the wound,
finding something yellow,
not blood but pollen, the full load
of the bee that hit him
on its way back to the hive,
reckless with a kind of joy, maybe,
having swung in the bells of a hundred blossoms
or gone blind in the wicker-work shadows of leaves.

Each day he wore it
like the smear of a clumsy kiss,
because it wouldn't wash off entirely,
though after it finally faded away,
he could touch the spot precisely
with the tip of his little finger,
an invisible button he pushed
to make his marrow hum,
to imagine himself honeyed and alive
in a bee-sung world,
not special or charged with an obscure purpose,
just someone other than he was,
better, he hoped.

MINDING

Because the insomniac lilac
thrashed the house all night,
I cut it back this morning,
laying its wind-twitchy limbs on the lawn,
not for punishment but to release
the nested restlessness,
leaving only a few stumps,
each stub bruised lavender,
and a half-dozen limber branches
like the kind my mother
used to make me break
and bring to her for switches
whenever I was bad,
the sting still in my legs
these long years since,
bucking me awake like voltage.

THE PASSED

Already it is later . . .
and now a little later . . .
and now later still.

This moment becomes
that moment—the one
you prayed for or feared
or never thought you'd see.

But you made it,
and again you made it,
and again . . .

Well, congratulations!
Even if you're bored, well done!
Whatever the distance between
the way it was and your expectations,
just getting there was an accomplishment.
Three cheers and then
three cheers and then . . .

Better not to start
the endless mariachi.
Just quietly commend yourself
in the moment for which
you immediately deserve commendation
because already it is over.

FOR THE EGO

Remember, life chose you,
not the other way around,
became a guest in your home,
a lavish relative en route somewhere else,
who, traveling light, can be off
before you've had a chance to say good-bye
or realized you aren't going along.
Go ahead, be hopeful
or, if it suits you, despair.
Pray to the undifferentiated consciousness
or shuffle off to the vacant end.
Either way, the option is
death of the self,
so that the question becomes,
which concept of annihilation
do you want to tuck you in
when you lie down each night with your
autonomic nervous system?

Nothing is a condition of namelessness,
ineffable emptiness waiting for a word,
for the spent breath of a moment
already expiring.
Call it a life *and* death situation;
call it anything you like;
call up a friend; call someone at random;
call through the screen door at twilight,
"Come here, boy, come here";
call all the animals out of the void;
populate the globe with names;
name the space to either side of you
into which you dangle your arms;
name yourself to yourself:
O house of bones;
O sweet, ephemeral one!

THE PHILOSOPHY OF METAPHOR

Out of the need to know comes
a kind of understanding, not answers,
as when the philosopher responds,
"We yearn for God because we need God,"
but you had asked an entirely different question.

God is and God is not
are the same order of belief,
cloister of the infinite clause,
like running forward or backward in place—
there you are, pounding the common ground.

In the equation $1 = 1$,
which 1 would you rather be?
Or say the choice is $1 = 0$;
does anything change
when you are what you are?

Look in the mirror and you see
what you look like
looking in the mirror.
Wave and you see yourself waving
to see yourself wave.

It could go on like this for a long time,
so imagine someone hands you a stone,
saying, "Take this flower."
Doesn't the whole craggy cliffside
break into bloom?

DUSK

This last, late light
reminds me of some lost moment,
a shimmer, a shiver,
as when the spine surprises
with a sudden shudder and someone says,
"A rabbit ran across your grave."

Just a mood, a mote in the blood
passing through the ventricle
and dispersed, one more
near-recognition to ignore,
inexpressible, anyway,
hardly worth mentioning.

If you say you understand,
we will share a moment of vacancy,
like strangers stopped in separate cars,
side by side on the jammed freeway,
alone in the stalled onrush,
though we have such light in common.

FLIGHT

The river slops under the bridge,
rubs the muddy turn of the bank
and glistens in sunlight,
straightaway and brilliant as a landing strip.

Call it a kind of redemption,
the way the simple light purifies,
though any dipped cup comes back so murky
no one could gag it down—
a failure of vision, let's say,
too much common sense—
the rim just touching the lips.

A quick gulp would reveal
what the heron knows.
At such a thought,
the stomach jumps like a fish;
but already the sun has shifted,
and whatever winged thing lingered there
has flown.

MIGRATORY PATTERNS

The past hangs on,
a bit of shell stuck
in the down of the new life.
Pecked at and swallowed,
it enters what it once contained,
becomes pulse and bone
and lifts into a sky.

This is how we come home,
steering the steep retreats,
by star, by marrow light,
the toppled years beneath,
a continent of ruin.

Indelible, the old coordinates—
town, street, number,
a tree by a window—
even razed and paved over,
the true ground pulling,
and in the air a fluttering.